ROOM *for* IMPROVEMENT

using nonstructural means, leaving major work until the children are older.

The future: Major structural work is the sort of thing most people only want to experience once. Think about the future. Might you need more than one extra bedroom within the next five to ten years? Try to get everything done at the same time.

When you have the answer to these questions, solving problems will be easier because you'll have a framework. If adding on is out of the question because of the cost, you'll be able to spend time considering other possibilities. Or, if you can afford to add on, you'll be able to start thinking about the type and size of home addition needed.

Consider how the house is used by you and your family. You will probably find that some rooms are used more than others. Children, for instance, may ignore their bedroom during the day, preferring to play downstairs in an already overcrowded living room. Perhaps the bedroom is cold, or uncomfortable, or badly equipped for play. Ensuring that heating is efficient, installing smooth cushioned vinyl flooring (a good surface for toy cars, model railways and games) and adding a work surface, portable TV and some storage space could put a swift end to the discomfort of trying to relax against a background of Space Invaders and squabbles. Another solution could be to convert the attic into a playroom.

Location of rooms is important too. A corridor between a dining room and kitchen can make serving meals difficult. A child's bedroom sited at the front of the house, where there is noise from the street and from the living room immediately below can cause sleeping problems.

Look at the size and shape of the rooms and list the features you like or dislike about each one. Think about light. Would a bigger window, a change of color scheme or a mullioned door help?

Does the decoration suit the purpose of the room? Children's rooms should have either washable (vinyl) paper or latex paint on the walls. Wallpaper tends to peel in a steamy bathroom.

Perhaps the problem is simply one of style. Rooms with no identify, packed with a jumble of furniture and with no decorative theme make a home that looks and feels disorganized. An eclectic mixture of objects can work, provided the objects are attractive in themselves. Style is a matter of personal preference. Think about the things you like. It's likely they'll be similar in design. Once you've established this and eliminated the things you hate, you are well on the way to establishing a home that works as a whole. When you've assessed what is wrong and how much you can afford to put right, go back to your problems chart and add the solutions that you have decided upon.

Left: *A folding table provides dining space in this small kitchen. The side leaves are let down and the table is put aside when not in use.*

Left: *A glass-topped table occupies less visual space than one with a solid top and makes a bridge between kitchen and dining areas.*

CHANGING SPACES

LIFE ON THE LEVELS

The conventional arrangement of upstairs and downstairs isn't the only way to divide rooms. This modern house was built into a cliffside, and designed to work on several interconnecting levels. The house has no ordinary interior doors; instead all the rooms have sliding doors, framed in pine. The whole interior is an exercise in intelligent use of space, and is packed with ideas to inspire.

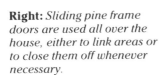

Right: *Sliding pine frame doors are used all over the house, either to link areas or to close them off whenever necessary.*

Below: *This staircase leads from the lower level to the loft living room.*

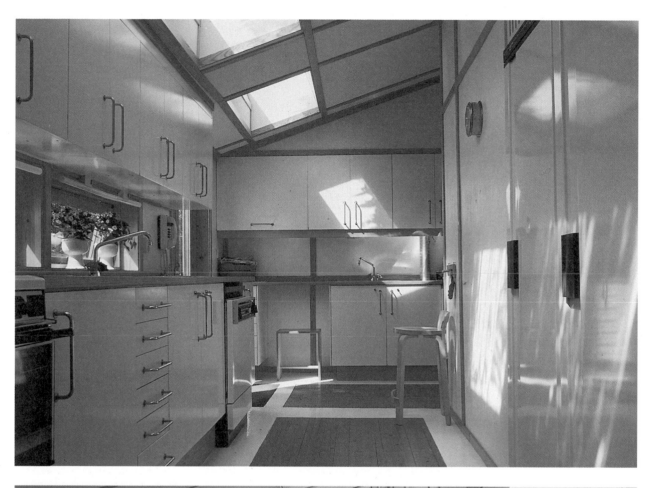

Left: *There's no space wasted in this kitchen. Light comes through the roof, and from narrow strips of glass set between wall and base cabinets.*

Left: *Windows at ceiling level flood the living room with light. A minimum of furniture makes the most of the long, narrow space.*

FINDING AN EXPERT

If you decide to use an architect or builder, the next step is to find someone properly qualified to do the work.

ARCHITECTS

A good architect will discuss your ideas, point out any pitfalls, then transform them into a design that suits both your style and your pocket. The best way to find an architect is by word of mouth. Barring that, contact the nearest office of the American Institute of Architects for referrals to qualified architects in your area. Be prepared to explain your needs so that the AIA can match you up with an architect who is qualified to do the kind of work you have in mind. Another approach is to find an addition you like and ask the home-owner who the architect was who designed it. As you search for an architect, beware of un-qualified architects, who may describe them-selves as "architectural designers" or "design consultants." An unqualified architect can cause disaster, so be careful and make your choice through official sources.

Once you have a list of names, contact the architects and explain the sort of building you have in mind. Ask what kind of work they have done and whether it is possible to see a local example. Ask about fees too. Most ar-chitects charge by the hour for the initial stages (although some will offer this advice free of charge in the hoipe that you will like the design and offer the firm the job). If you decide to see the architect to design, plan and oversee the work, the fee is usually a per-centage of the total building cost. The fee in-cludes design, drawing and presentation of plans, and may include finding a builder and supervising the construction. Don't choose the first architect you see. It's better to visit a few and find one whose ideas you like.

BUILDERS

Everyone knows a builder horror story. Tales of builders who disappear for weeks on end, leaving the job half done, shoddy workman-ship and overcharing are common. Firms like this are the exception rather than the rule, and a few elementary precautions at the early stages will protect you.

Personal recommendation is the best way to find a good builder. If you are using an ar-chitect, or or she may be able to recommend a firm whose work he or she knows. Neighbors and friends are another good source of information.

There are various professional organiza-tions of building contractors, and these can be a good source of referrals if your architect or friends have no suggestions. Among these are the Associated General Contractors of America, the Master Builders Association and the American Building Contractors As-sociation. Contact your local library for the national headquarters or for local branches. You might also phone your local office of the Better Business Bureau to see if their mem-bership includes any contractors.

In searching for a reputable contractor, make sure the candidates you are consider-ing are licensed and qualified to do the prop-osed work. Ask for references and don't be shy about following them up.

Make a shortlist of three or four builders and send them all a set of plans and a written specification (your architect will supply these) and ask for a written estimate and a schedule of when the work would begin and how it would progress. Allow three or four weeks for the estimates to come in.

Once the estimates have been received, you can choose the builder offering the best service and value for money. Take warranties into account when assessing the estimates. It is better to use the builder with the warranty, even if his estimate is a little more expensive than the others. Also ask to see the builder's insurance certificate to make sure that he has liability coverage. If he doesn't and a brick falls through your neighbor's greenhouse (or worse still, on his head), a nasty legal wrangle could ensue.

When the choice has been made and plans approved by the local building office, you must draw up a contract between you and your builder. This is essential and is your protection should something go wrong at a later stage. Word of mouth, or a confirming letter is not good enough.

The contract should specify every aspect of the work, from starting date to the materials to be used. A penalty clause may sound severe but the builder is more likely to finish on time if he will lose money by going beyond the agreed date. Your architect or lawyer will help with the contract.

Organize how interim payments will be made before the work starts – and don't part with any cash in advance. Equally, don't make the final payment until you are happy with the work. Above all, be firm. You are pay-ing. The builder is not doing you a favor by turning up or by doing the work as specified in the estimate.

SUPERVISING THE WORK

It will probably take between four to six weeks to reach a starting date, so there's plenty of time to clear the rooms affected by building work. Dust spreads everywhere, so remove carpets from the rooms around the new addition. Remember that the workmen will need somewhere to store tools, lunch facilities and a toilet.

If you are employing an architect, he will probably supervise the work. If you are supervising the work, make sure the builder knows where to contact you at all times.

CHECKPOINTS

A home addition is a big project, so bear the following in mind.

▶ If you are using an architect and don't like the first design submitted, say so. You have to live with the new building, use it and pay for it.

▶ Make sure the new building suits the style of your house. An addition that is an eyesore, or just plain unattractive, will make the house hard to sell.

▶ If you are adding a kitchen or bathroom, choose the fixtures before the addition is planned. It is easier to plan a new space to suit the cabinets or fixtures you really want than it is to make the fixtures work in a building of the wrong size or shape. And make due allowance for manufacturers' delivery dates, bearing in mind that it is possible that these will not necessarily be met.

▶ Go for the biggest space you can afford. Eventually you are sure to want more cabinets or equipment, and if you think big now, you will have the space when you need it.

▶ Make sure the new space does not reduce light to the rest of the house or make access inconvenient.

CONVERSIONS

ROOM ON TOP?

Most homeowners would deny wasting any usable space, and would be astonished to be told that there's a whole room standing empty above their heads, or at least the scope for creating such a room. When there isn't room to add on at street level, or when the need is for a quiet spot, away from the rest of the house, the roof space can offer a wealth of interesting possibilities. Conversion can be as simple as the addition of skylights (windows set into the roof), a floor, ceiling and access, or more complex with dormer windows to extend the usable floor area inside the attic. If the house is of suitable construction, it may even be possible to add an extra story, though you will need planning permission for such a venture and it is a very expensive one.

An attic room can be used as a bedroom, a second bathroom, a bedroom with a bathroom or shower room suite if there is enough space, a playroom, hobbies area or even a small apartment. Because the attic is quiet and well away from the main part of the house, conversion is the ideal way to make a retreat where parents can create an area of their own, children can play without causing chaos in the living room and teenagers can entertain friends, play music and watch TV without the inevitable disputes with the rest of the family. If one of the family has the kind of hobby that occupies a lot of space, the attic can become a tailor-made home for the model railroad, amateur radio rig, sewing, painting or pottery project.

An attic room is not, however, usually suitable for a grandparent's apartment. Elderly people may find the stairs difficult or could be worried about being cut off from the family when living at the top of the house. If a grandparent's room is needed, convert ground- or second-floor rooms and use the attic for younger, fitter members of the family.

Even the simplest attic conversion affects the structure of the roof, so design must be carried out by an architect or structural engineer, and the work done by a builder experienced in attic conversion.

Not all buildings can be extended at roof level. Obviously, a flat-roofed building has no attic space to convert, but it may be possible to add an extra story. Many modern houses where the roof is of trussed rafter construction (*see diagram*) cannot be extended. To extend an attic where the roof is built like this means removing the roof itself and doing a great deal of expensive support work. The

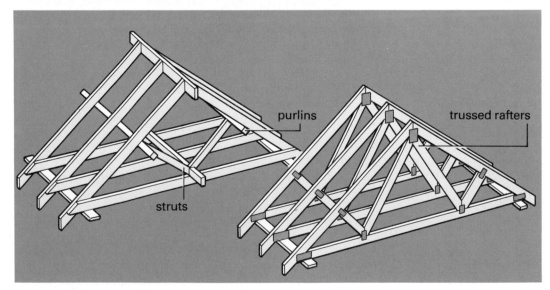

older style roof (*see diagram*) is ideal for attic conversion. If the house is of historic interest, or in a conservation area, planning permission for adding simple skylights, converting the attic with dormers or adding an extra floor may be refused. Check before contacting an architect or engineer.

Left: *Here, roofspace has been converted into a spacious second bathroom. Water-resistant wall-coverings have been used; textured tiles, vinyl wallpaper and tongue-and-groove cladding on the sloping ceiling. Twin rooflights let in the sun.*

Right: *A self-contained apartment with trap-door access, this pine-clad loft conversion makes maximum use of every inch – notice the cupboards in the eaves.*

Below left: *This is an older-style roof construction, suitable for loft conversion.*

Below right: *A roof with trussed rafters is not suitable for conversion. This style is common to modern houses.*

WINDOW SEATS

There's something wonderfully comforting about a window seat filled with plump, colorful cushions.

Building a window seat is an easy way to add an attractive feature to a room with bay windows, and there's a bonus as the space beneath the seat can be used for storage, accessible either through a hinged top or from doors at the front.

Like most good ideas, window seats are simple to make and well within the scope of a do-it-yourselfer equipped with an electric drill and screwdriver. Build a frame from wood, then add ready-made panels to the front. Louver doors can be used, or replacement wooden kitchen doors (available from home improvement stores in cathedral arch and fielded panel styles). If the top is to be covered by a padded seat, make it from chipboard. If the top will be seen, use 1½- to 2-inch-thick wood. Use a router to make a rounded edge at the front, then stain both the seat and top to match the front. If you buy plain louvers or doors, they can be stained to almost any color or wood effect.

If a radiator has been installed under a window where you might want to build a window seat, double glazing the window will mean the radiator can be positioned elsewhere in the room.

A deep window recess or other alcove can be turned into a miniature spare bedroom. All you need to do is build a base wide enough to take a single size mattress and hang curtains so that they pull across the front of the space to give some privacy. The mattress can be concealed with a slipcover made from upholstery fabric (quilted fabric looks effective) and throw cushions for day-to-day use. If you are building a bed in an alcove, add some narrow shelves to act as a bedside table.

THE LINEN CLOSET

In many homes the linen closet already is a multi-purpose repository for towels, sheets, tablecloths and even sundries like toothpaste, shampoo, soap and toilet paper. But there may still be more effective ways to use the space. See if any of the add-on storage accessories can mobilize inaccessible corners. Clip-on wire baskets, for example, can double your storage by making full use of the space below shelves. These baskets are available at good department stores in various sizes. Slide two baskets underneath each shelf and use the space below to stack towels, etc. Small baskets attached to the inside of the door will make it a good storage spot for toiletries and cleaning materials.

The inside of the linen closet door can be a good place to store the ironing board and iron, or the vacuum cleaner. Storage racks for ironing boards and irons are available from good department stores. These days, a vacuum cleaner may even come supplied with a hanging kit.

Of course, a small, shallow linen closet built into a hall wall may simply be the best use of space – in which case, organization will be your best friend.

Left: *Window seats should be cozy corners where you can curl up with a good book, or sit gazing at the view outside. Painted in shades of sunshine yellow, this delightful niche has the added attraction of underseat storage.*

BE SPACE-EFFICIENT

There's no truer saying than the old maxim "a place for everything and everything in its place". Clutter will make a small home seem even smaller. Cleaning materials, makeup, shoes, magazines and toys are difficult to store when there's no obvious place to put them. The answer is to look for under-used areas. Hang storage baskets on the backs of doors. Inside closets, they can be used for shoes, for makeup in the bathroom and for small toys in children's rooms. Hanging tiers of wire baskets are equally useful for kitchen odds and ends, fruit and vegetables, toiletries and the bits of broken toys, car wheels and old crayons most children seem unable to live without. Consider adding floor-to-ceiling shelves in hallways if there is enough width. Don't ignore the space under the bed. Either buy a storage bed (*see bedrooms section*), or invest in some plastic boxes on castors so that sheets, pillowcases, toys or shoes can be easily within reach.

If it is an effort to put things away, people will tend to find excuses not to be tidy. The best place to store anything is close to the place where that object is most often used, in a space that is easy to get in and out of.

Finding the space for storage may not seem easy in a small house, so think about the less obvious areas. Tall, narrow cabinets set at either side of a door with a shelf or matching bridging cupboard running over the top are unobtrusive and will hold a surprisingly large amount. If space is really tight, replace conventional doors with pull-down blinds suspended from the ceiling.

In a small bathroom, it will probably be worth replacing the basin with one which can be built into a counter with a cabinet beneath. There isn't much space around most bathtubs, but take a look, especially at the end opposite the faucet. If there is a useful area, build a small cabinet to fit the space, and attach a hinged door to hide the contents. Use the cabinet for cleaning materials. It will also be worth adding shelves above the bath to use for toiletries and towels. Glass shelves look attractive and won't be too badly affected by steam. But take care not to put shelves where you might bang into them when getting into or out of the bath. Make sure that glass shelves (or indeed any shelves) are firmly attached to their supporting brackets or studs so they cannot be accidentally dislodged.

Above all, never say "there isn't room." There is . . . if you look for it.

SPACE-SAVING DOORS

Doors which open into a room are restricting when space is limited. The area behind the hinged side of the door cannot be used and the floor area in front needs to be clear. There are various types of space-saving doors available.

Bi-folds: Bi-fold doors hinge at the center and fold one against the other. A typical bi-fold is about a third of the width of a conventional opening door. Their only disadvantage is that when open they project a small amount into the room. They still allow better access than hinged doors in crowded areas and take up less floor space.

Concertina doors: Concertina folding doors are pleated if made from fabric, or divided into narrow sections if made from a solid material. When the door is opened, the sections push together to lie flat against the door frame.

Sliding doors: A sliding door can be installed so that it slides along the wall adjacent to the doorway. This does mean that this section of wall cannot be used for anything else.

Shutters: Pull-down shutters are usually only seen in offices and industrial buildings but can look effective in the home. Wooden shutter doors have a warmer, friendlier feel than the metal type.

Curtaining: The cheapest solution is to remove the door and replace it with a curtain hung from a track fitted at the top of the door frame. The curtain fabric can be light in the summer and thick in winter.

Facing page: Bi-fold doors consist of hinged panels which concertina as the door is opened. They do project a small amount into the room. The louvered type look good with this bathroom.

Far left: The bathroom with its original door. See how much floor space the door takes up with its opening arc.

Left: Concertina doors are the simplest of all to install, since they only have one top track. Unlike bi-folds, they don't project beyond the width of the frame or protrude into the room space.

Below: Rigid sliding doors are ideal provided there is enough room to one side of the opening for them to slide open. This tiny bathroom suddenly becomes much more accessible.

Pattern is important to the success of a color scheme, adding visual relief in the same way as splashes of color. If, for instance, you have decided to paint the walls pale pink, and have selected a gray carpet and upholstery, using plain pink or gray curtains would be a safe, but dull, choice. Look instead for a pattern. You might, in this instance, choose curtain and pillow fabric with a gray background, patterned in pink, blue, cream or gray shades. Add pink accessories, or break up the floor area with a plain or patterned rug and a static scheme has warmth and life. Repetition is an important part of any successful scheme. Picking up upholstery colors in piping, on cushions or curtain tie-backs may seem fussy, but it is this attention to detail that makes the difference between a pleasant room and one that attracts admiring comments.

Patterns can be used together, providing they are of the same basic design. You could, for instance, use a smaller version of the pattern on upholstery for curtains and lampshades. Avoid using patterns that "fight" with one another. Unless carefully chosen, a heavily patterned carpet, wallcovering and upholstery can be disastrous. Bold pattern can be used as a single focal point in an otherwise plain room. Remember that pattern does not necessarily mean fabric. Carved woodwork, textured blinds, loosely woven upholstery and architectural details all add pattern to a room. A simple way to accentuate the pattern of a cornice or molding is to paint it in a deeper or paler shade than the rest of the walls. Sometimes, pattern can be the starting point for a color scheme, when a particular wallpaper or fabric is the dominant element.

Light can add pattern too. Sunlight streaming through a venetian blind, or a table lamp shining through the leaves of a well-established plant can do as much to enliven a plain wall as a patterned wallcovering. A pleated lampshade will produce a different effect than a plain one in the same color.

Never rush headlong into a color scheme. You will have to live with the results for quite a long time, so tread carefully until you are sure that the combination of color and pattern is the right one. Making a color board will help. Some paint manufacturers sell small sample cans of paint, so you can try it out on a small area of wall (paint always looks different up than it does in the can or on the shade card). It is better to invest in one roll of wallpaper, stick a length up and decide you don't like it, than to discover you and the pattern can't live happily together once all the paper has been paid for. But ask the wallpaper salesperson to hold the requisite total number of rolls while you try the first one. Otherwise you could find the remainder comes from another dye batch and doesn't quite match up. Study room schemes in magazines and make a file of those you like. It is likely that they will all be of one type, a clue to the sort of schemes you will be comfortable with.

USING STRIPES

Wallcovering can have a dramatic visual effect on a room, particularly if the pattern runs in a distinctive direction.

Everyone knows that vertical stripes will make a room seem higher while horizontal lines will make the space seem lower and sometimes wider.

In practice, it isn't quite as simple as that. Thin stripes in a soft color on a white or neutral background have a better effect than wide, boldly colored stripes. Diagonal stripes, particularly if they are incorporated into a trellis pattern, widen space and are a good idea for the short walls in a narrow room.

The color you choose for paint and wallpaper can alter the apparent size of the room. The cool colors – blues, pale greens, lilacs and misty grays – recede, pushing back

the walls of a small room. This is why thin, soft gray stripes work better than the much more assertive bright red ones.

ON THE BORDER

Wallpaper borders provide tremendous scope for the creative decorator. They can be used to add interest to plain walls where a room is too small to stand strong pattern; add definition when used around the edge of a sloping ceiling or make tall, featureless walls seem lower and more interesting when added as a dado rail at waist height.

Borders can be run along the top of walls as a substitute for cornice. If the walls are very high, position the border at picture rail height (about 18 inches) below the level of the ceiling. This can also distract attention from an uneven ceiling line. Decorate the space above to match the ceiling. Many modern border designs have been made to look like stencils, a boon for those who aren't confident or artistic enough to attempt the real thing themselves.

Using a border is a good way to mark the dividing line between different patterns, or between paint and patterned wallcovering. Apply the border at waist height and run it up the sides and around the top of any doors or windows in the room. Use paint, either sponged or stippled on the lower half of the wall and a complementary patterned wallpaper above. The new coordinated collections of wallcoverings, borders and paint make this sort of mixing and matching well within the scope of the adventurous amateur home decorator.

Left: *Bold striped wallpaper could be overpowering if used on every wall, but here it is seen to best effect, broken up by closets, reflected by a mirror and making the ceilings of this small room look much higher than they are. The crisp, cool atmosphere of the room has been achieved by the use of blue and white, both rather cold colors. Extra warmth comes from the glowing brass bed frame and the gold trim on the fittings.*

THE ART OF ILLUSION

Don't be cast into despair if there's no structural rescue for a small, dark or awkwardly shaped room. Clever use of color, pattern, mirrors, light and texture can work wonders with the most unpromising location. Simplicity is the key. Remember, clutter crowds and dark colors have the effect of drawing walls inward. Pale colors, simple patterns and well-organized space have the opposite effect. Choose semigloss paint, as it has a slightly shiny surface that will reflect light and make the room seem bigger.

The quickest, easiest transformation for a small room is to paint the walls in a pale color and re-cover upholstery to match. Pale needn't mean white. Tinted white paints (whites with a hint of rose, yellow, blue or green) are all good. So are the very palest shades of yellow, blue, green and gray, the cool colors. Pale pinks, apricot, lavender and brown are warm colors and have the opposite effect. Use variations of the main shade for upholstery in self-patterned or textured fabric for a look that's cool and calm.

Pattern can create space, providing you choose the right type. Vertical stripes will make a low-ceilinged room seem higher. Diagonal lines have the effect of pushing walls outward and are particularly good used in carpeting. Pale trellis designs have a 3D effect. Most wallpaper manufacturers have a trellis in their line, or you can paint ordinary garden trellis white and attach it to an end wall in a rectangular room. Leaf green looks wonderful behind painted trellis.

As well as these simple tricks, there are more complex and effective ways to give the illusion of space.

Above: *Always position mirrors so that the reflection is interesting. This series of mirrored sliding-door closets reflects the room facing. Placing mirror at right angles to a window, as here, has the effect of visually lengthening the room. Big green plants add a cool, spacious air.*

MIRROR MAGIC

When Alice stepped through the looking glass, she found another room. In real life, the room itself won't be beyond the mirror, but you can exploit the illusion to add both space and light.

A wall of mirrored glass, cleverly placed, can give the impression that the room is longer, wider or that there is another room beyond. Mirror attached at right angles or opposite a window increases light. Arched mirror panels placed along a wall at evenly spaced intervals will suggest that the room leads on to more space.

Large pieces of mirror glass were once only available to interior decorators and the trade. Happily, this has changed and most home improvement centers now stock tall mirror panels in various widths, mirror arches and mirror tiles. Various finishes are available, including plain silvered, smoked, bronze veined and even etched glass.

Mirror panels and tiles are easy to install. Some small mirrors have self-adhesive pads on the back; others are attached to the wall using mirror screws, clips, adhesive or wood. Packs bought at home improvement centers come with full instructions.

Wherever you put mirror panels, make sure that the reflection works well; otherwise the illusion will be destroyed. Avoid reflecting posters or books – writing will be back to front. Likewise, steer clear of seating areas as most people find it disturbing to be constantly aware of their mirror image. Plants or a small table displaying an interesting object are both good subjects for reflection.

Mirror tiles only work well if the backing wall is completely flat. A bumpy wall will make it impossible to align the tiles, giving crooked, visually disturbing lines. Mount mirror panels on wood strips instead.

Left: *You can make a short, narrow area such as a hallway seem twice as long by positioning a mirror at the end. Here mirror doors conceal a useful storage closet and visually lengthen the hall.*

PART TWO

ROOM-BY-ROOM IMPROVEMENTS

Small Wonders, page 86

Bedroom Basics, page 146

THE CONTEMPORARY KITCHEN

Less than 80 years ago many women only set foot in their own kitchen in order to tell someone else what to do. Men, on the whole, remained in total ignorance of the goings on there.

In stark contrast to this was the life of many thousands of poor families, for whom the kitchen was also the living room and sometimes a bedroom too. The only facilities in the average working class kitchen were a cold water tap and a coal-fired range.

Today, the kitchen is a family room, used by everyone from toddlers upward. The head cook and maid of the early 1900s have been replaced by a battery of high tech, super-efficient appliances designed to make cooking and cleaning up afterwards easy, and only the rich have the luxury of a cook.

Kitchens have more than kept up with the fast pace of change over the past 80 years. Most homes have a modern range, a refrigerator and freezer and an automatic washing machine and dryer, with microwaves and dishwashers gaining in popularity. Some even include built-in toasters, coffee makers and food processors.

Skilled European designers lead the field in innovative kitchen design. As well as being smart on the outside, today's cabinets are packed with clever storage gadgetry on the inside. For those working to a very tight budget, but with some experience of assembling unit furniture, there are good self-assembly kits available. Mass production has brought ceramic tiling, once very expensive, within reach and there are paints, fabrics and floorings to match or complement every style of kitchen cabinet.

With so much to choose from, remodeling a kitchen can be difficult. It pays to shop around. Collect together as many manufacturer's brochures as you can. Study the way the rooms shown are designed, as well as the style of the cabinets. Most have good ideas that you could adapt to improve the kitchen you already have if you are not keen to spend the amount of money an all-new kitchen requires.

Installing a new kitchen is an expensive business, so don't rush in and live to regret your haste later. Making a list, like the one shown below, may seem a tedious business, but if you calculate your needs with as much accuracy as possible at this stage it can save you time and expense in the long run.

In this section, you will find ideas on improving what you have.

Above and right: *Both views of this kitchen show how much pass-through room has been allowed due to clever planning. Set-back wall cabinets allow improved headroom.*

ASSESS YOUR KITCHEN NEEDS

Your lifestyle
► What do you dislike about your present kitchen?

► Which features would you keep?

► If you could have your ideal kitchen, what would it look like?

► How many people use the kitchen at one time?

► Do pets use the kitchen?

Eating
► Do you want to eat in the kitchen?

► If so, which meals and for how many?

► What sort of table would you like (breakfast bar, pull out, or permanent table).

Activities
► What is the kitchen used for?

► Which activities cause you the biggest problem? If the answer is laundry, for instance, think about building a laundry room elsewhere.

Budget
► How much can you afford to spend?

► How will you raise the money (bank, savings and loan, etc).

► Are you thinking of moving within the next few years? If you are, spending a lot on a kitchen will be a waste.
Redecorate and install good-quality budget-priced cabinets instead.

Appliances
► Do you entertain a lot? This will affect the size and type of appliances you buy.

Space
► Is there enough space to make the improvement you want? If not, think about employing an architect or builder, either to find extra space within the existing structure, or to plan an extension.

► Do you need a dishwasher, a microwave, a deep fat fryer or food processor? They all take up space.

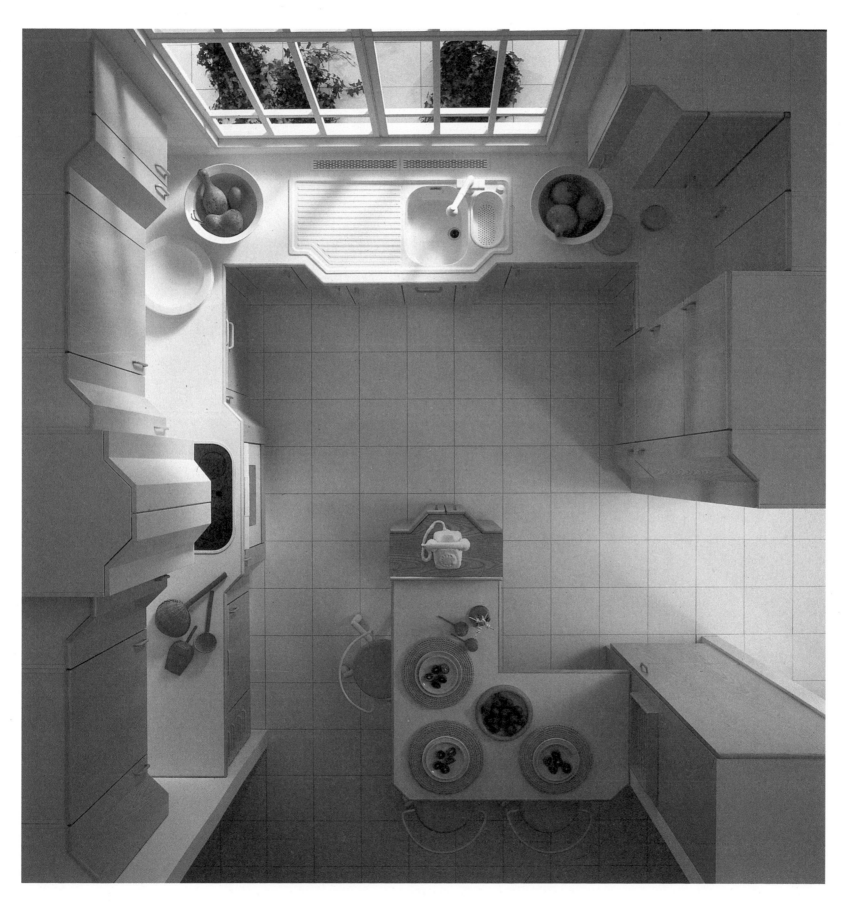

weight in gold, able to cope with everything from making eggs for breakfast to drying damp clothes and generating extra heat. Try to find space for a separate laundry room where the family can dump dirty linen and where there is enough space to iron and hang clothes.

CREATING A STYLE

For the room to work as a whole, kitchen fittings, dining and relaxing furniture should be in harmony. Country style, with pine cabinets, a big stripped table, wheelback chairs, a dresser and a settee or friendly chintz sofa strewn with colorful cushions or an afghan has a timeless appeal. Pine kitchen cabinets are easy to find, but look for wood in a mellow, aged shade. Counters should ideally be tiled or wooden, but these can be impractical materials in a family kitchen. Look for a laminate in a natural stone, tile or burlap effect and add wood molding. Choose wall tiles in warm, country colors in a slightly bumpy "hand-made" finish, or mix old-fashioned junk shop finds with plains. Forget about coordination. So long as you stick to natural effects, you'll achieve the eclectic "grew with time" look of a real farmhouse kitchen.

A big range will add a comforting country touch, but for layout convenience you may prefer a separate cooktop and ovens. Happily, you can still achieve a country style. Many appliances are available in brown, gold or cream, all better colors for the country look (and less likely to show sticky fingerprints) than conventional white.

A wall-hung collection of transfer-printed plates or prints, dried flowers or bunches of herbs suspended from the ceiling and a hutch to display a favorite collection of jugs or traditional china are basic elements in the country kitchen. Wicker baskets, either hanging from the ceiling or stacked in piles of different sizes against a wall will add to the rustic atmosphere. But take care that any items hung from the ceiling are above head-height, do not have sharp edges and are properly secured. Children will appreciate a painted chest or a pine coffer to keep favorite toys close at hand.

A nice way to add to the family atmosphere is to attach a cork bulletin board to the wall with a picture light or down beam spotlight above and fill it with favorite family snapshots, shopping lists and reminders.

It is more difficult to achieve a warm, friendly effect with modern kitchen furniture, but possible if you choose a line that includes matching or complementary dining furniture, storage and seating. The high tech look, with its bright, easy-to-clean surfaces copes well with family life. You'll need the same elements as described in the country kitchen: somewhere to eat, somewhere to relax, functional, practical appliances and storage.

Whatever your style, avoid creating a room which is difficult to clean. Rustic, bare bricks look wonderful with old pine furniture but quickly collect airborne grease. Pale upholstery will soon look the worse for wear where there are small children, as will a beautiful hand-painted traditional kitchen. Think of your family kitchen as a cross between workroom, playroom, living room and office and the activities it will be used for. The easiest way to plan is to make a list of all the things you hope to do in the kitchen, then match facilities to the action. If you haven't room for all of them, at least it will help you to decide what are the priorities and perhaps to plan some dual-purpose amenities that might otherwise be overlooked until it is too late. Do not stint yourself at this stage; remember, you may never again have the opportunity to plan your dream kitchen. Your list might look something like this:

Below: *Creating desk space in your kitchen need not be a major undertaking. All you need do is adapt this clever design with its flap-down desk-top.*

ACTIVITY	AMENITY
▶ Cooking family meals	Big, efficient range and freezer Microwave Dishwasher
▶ Playspace for toddlers	Soft, easy-to-clean floor Storage for favorite toys Space for playpen or highchair Table to use for drawing and games First aid kit Pan guard for cooktop Lock for freezer
▶ Entertaining friends	Comfortable seating Big table to seat six or more
▶ Home office	Desk space (an area of countertop with a filing cabinet on castors is ideal) Bulletin board Phone and message pad (should be within reach of the cooking area)
▶ Eating	Dining area and comfortable chairs
▶ Relaxing	TV and radio Comfortable seating Relaxing lighting. Use table lamps to create pools of light around the seating area.

SMALL WONDERS

Clever planning is a must for a small or awkwardly shaped kitchen where it is vital to make good use of every inch of space. Standard-sized cabinets and appliances may prove impossible to fit, so you will need to think of alternatives, or use a kitchen planner, depending on your budget.

Look carefully at the space before you start buying cabinets or appliances. Measure it and draw up a plan on graph paper. There may be obvious ways to gain extra space: by removing a chimney breast, or taking the doors off a built-in cupboard. Make a list of the appliances you want to include and the things you need to store.

SPACE-SAVING EQUIPMENT

Equipment is the "bones" of the kitchen and must come first in your calculations. Do you really need a full-size stove? A compact all-in one stove/microwave or stove/dishwasher will meet the needs of a single person or a couple. A cooktop with a hinge-down cover will give you extra worksurface. Many space-saving small appliances are now available in small, under-cabinet models. Others combine several functions into one, like a microwave/toaster-oven. A dishwasher is worth having if there is space because it cuts down on clutter and will help to keep work-

Above: *When space is difficult or very restricted, special-sized cabinets can usually provide the answer to the problem of designing a working kitchen. This kitchen has been planned around the sloping ceiling. Instead of being mounted above the counter, the wall cabinets sit on top of it and have a useful shelf running around the top. The European modular cabinets can be moved around as wished.*

surfaces free of dirty dishes when you are preparing food. A compact refrigerator/ freezer takes up less space and may be adequate for your needs, especially if you don't store large quantities of perishable food. If laundry equipment must be in the kitchen, a stacking washer and dryer occupy less space than separate appliances.

CABINETS AND STORAGE

If the kitchen is narrow, standard size cabinets will probably eat up too much floor area. This won't be a difficulty if money is no object as you can call on the expertise of a kitchen planner or have a custom-built kitchen. Many major kitchen cabinet manufacturers produce narrower cabinets or 3D cabinets where the doors are angled back from full to just over half width, corner mounted cabinets and midway shelving. Combined with the skills of a kitchen planner, these special-sized units can turn the smallest, most awkward kitchen into a well-designed, functional room.

For those on a tight budget, planning a small kitchen needs ingenuity and an imaginative approach to space. If there is no room for conventional base cabinets, cut a worktop down and fit shelves with bi-fold or sliding doors beneath, and use tiers of wire baskets on castors for drawers. Install narrow shelves in place of wall cabinets and either leave them open, or cover with bi-fold doors or roller blinds. Under-shelf baskets will increase the storage capacity of your shelves, or screw in some simple hooks for jugs, cups, etc. Provided that they are very stable, free-standing shelves can be used if you don't own a power drill, an essential when installing fixed shelving. Where there is not enough depth for a worktop of any sort, make the most of wall space with floor to ceiling shelves, just wide enough to house pots and pans. You will gain valuable space by replacing a conventional door with a pocket door, or by removing the door completely. A hinge-down or pull-out counter will add an eating area to the kitchen, or extra preparation space when needed.

Neatness is essential in a small kitchen. A build-up of clutter where space is already strained will make the room totally unworkable, so make sure utensils are hung up on rails or tidied away when finished with. Explore the possibility of storing rarely used kitchen equipment on top of cabinets or in any awkward gaps that may exist.

DECORATION

The right decor will make your small kitchen seem bigger. Choose light, shiny surfaces and steer clear of fussy patterns. In a confined space it may be necessary to put the stove quite close to the window – in which case blinds will not only be safer, but they will also look neater than curtains, or you can screen the window with glass shelves and plants. White, combined with a primary or pastel trim, is a guaranteed space maker. Use white shelves and counters with a primary edging and add matching colored handles to the cupboards and drawers. Spotlights mounted on ceiling track will bounce light off shiny surfaces, making the room appear larger, and can be adjusted at will.

Below: *A long, narrow kitchen is easy to plan if there is room for cabinets along both sides, as shown here. The task becomes more difficult when there is not enough space for facing rows of cabinets. A solution is to fill one wall with narrow shelves.*

treated so that they are heatproof. If you have small children, a wipe-clean lacquered or laminate table would be a practical choice.

Flooring needs to be practical, especially if you have children who may spill food on the carpet. Vinyl, ceramic or quarry tiles and wooden flooring look attractive and are easy-to-clean.

Lighting should be soft but bright enough for people to see what they are eating. A rise-and-fall pendant light gives just the right level of illumination and can be run from a dimmer switch when you want a soft background light to complement the glow of candles. The sideboard, hutch or serving area should be lit by wall lights.

The style of your dining area depends on personal taste if it is a separate room, and on the other furniture if it is part of a kitchen or living area. Eating should be a pleasurable experience and a good way to achieve the right feeling of relaxation and comfort is to think about restaurants you particularly like and adapt the look to suit your home.

Traditional style: Combine a fine old polished-wood table with matching chairs and sideboard, richly swathed curtains or drapes, dark warm colors, parquet flooring and an oriental rug. This style works well in a separate, high-ceilinged dining room, or in a living room where upholstered furniture is equally formal.

Farmhouse style: Best combined with a big pine kitchen. Look for a large scrubbed table (preferably old and original), a hutch and wheelback chairs. Terracotta or ceramic tile flooring and cottage prints are the perfect partners for this easy-to-live-with style. Can be combined with a living room if there is enough space for the table and the up-holstered furniture has chintz or cottage print covers.

Colonial classic: A good idea if you want style on a budget as wicker dining furniture is sensibly priced and looks wonderful with a stripped pine or woodblock floor, Indian rug, white walls and plenty of lush green plants. This look goes particularly well with simple, modern furniture.

High tech: Lovers of the dramatic can choose a stark black dining table and match-ing chairs; the more conventional will like the clean looks of blonde ash or oak. The table could also be a trestle style, with a glass top and brightly colored legs. This clean, unclut-tered look is good for a small room, or for a dining alcove off a modern living room.

DUAL-PURPOSE DINING ROOMS

In a home where space is valuable, you will need to make maximum use of every inch, in-cluding the dining room. Rule number one is not to have the traditional table surrounded by chairs. Look instead for a table which can be pulled away from the wall (where it can be used as a desk or for hobbies), and with extra leaves so that it can be extended for enter-taining. Instead of the traditional sideboard, opt for shelving with cupboard or drawer bases. Some cabinets have a fold down desk section which will save cluttering the table with books – and having to clear everything away when you want to eat. It is a good idea to keep homework or hobby equipment on a wheeled cart that can stand beside you as you work and be whisked away when the room is needed for meals.

In a large dining room, you can set up a hobby or homework corner and hide it with a folding screen when serving meals. Where there is enough space, a sofa bed is a useful addition, especially for guests who don't want to drive home after a leisurely, delicious meal – or rather too much to drink. Using the dining room as a spare bedroom for more than one or two nights is not a very comforta-ble arrangement for your guests.

You'll find a cart is a very useful addition in a dining room where shelving or base cabinets mean that there is no space for a sideboard to use as a shelving area. Choose a well-made, solid cart that pushes easily.

What to do with dining chairs can be a problem. You will need at least two in the room for the times when it is being used for hobbies or study. Folding chairs are best as they can be stored in a cupboard or hung on the wall when not in use. Heaving solid dining chairs from various locations in the house every time you want to eat is an activity which will soon pall.

Don't forget about lighting for your home office or hobby area. If you are using the main table, a rise-and-fall pendant will be fine. A floor-standing light, clip-on spot or angled table lamp is best if you have sectioned-off a corner for privacy and neatness.

MAKING A DINING ALCOVE

A dining alcove in a living room is the best way to separate the two areas without build-ing a wall. You may be lucky enough to have a natural alcove, in the bay of a window, the short arm of an L or the recess beside a chim-ney breast. If you have, capitalize on this and tuck your dining table and chairs as far back into it as you can (making sure people can still get in and out of their seats with ease). A bamboo screen would help to seal off the area from the rest of the room. An area like this provides many interesting decorative opportunities. If there is space, you could line the walls of the alcove with narrow book-shelves, or cover them floor-to-ceiling with a collection of plates or pictures. Stenciling around the outside edges of the alcove, or adding a dado rail painted to contrast or complement the walls will have the effect of setting your alcove in a frame. The walls can be painted in a paler or darker shade than the rest of the room, covered in a patterned wallpaper if the rest of the room is plain, or plain if it is patterned.

A good way to save space in a narrow alcove is to build padded benches against the wall instead of using chairs. All that is needed is a simple wooden frame which can then be covered with tongue and groove boarding or kitchen cabinet doors, stained to look like panels. Add a lift-up lid (the space beneath the bench can be used for storage) and a comfortable padded cushion upholstered in fabric to match or complement seating in the main part of the room.

One of the prettiest alcoves I have ever seen was screened with lavish pinch pleated drapes, plain on one side, patterned on the other and tied back with a braided rope of the two fabrics. Inside was a lovely oval walnut table, with padded benches covered to match the curtains built around the wall. The effect was lavish and wonderfully Edwardian, rather like a box at the theater, or a private restaurant room in an old hotel in England.

The alcove will need its own lighting. A rise-and-fall pendant is best but may be awk-ward in such a small space. Recessed ceiling downlighters controlled by dimmers and corner-mounted spotlights which can be directed onto the table are a good combina-tion. On special occasions, add a touch of romance with candles or a couple of old-fashioned oil lamps at each end of the table. While you are eating, lighting in the main part of the room can be reduced to a minimum, to give an increased feeling of intimacy.

Where there isn't an alcove, it is possible to create one by building a platform at one end of the room, or making the divide with low shelving or trellis. A collection of big indoor plants and a change of flooring from carpet to tiles or parquet is a simpler way to do the same thing.

ONE ROOM, THREE USES

Knocking a living room, dining area and kitchen into one is a bold step, but one big room cleverly divided by screens, plants, seating, shelving and furniture can often work better than three small rooms.

Not all houses are suitable for this sort of treatment. The ideal is a house from the 1930s, 1940s or 1950s, where the three rooms were often arranged either in a row or L-shaped with the kitchen forming the short leg of the L.

There must be natural light at both ends of the room. Don't be ruled by convention; the kitchen need not go at the backyard end but can be at the front of the house if you would rather plan your seating area where you can relax and look out at the greenery instead of the street.

If there is a hall running down the side of the kitchen and dining room, incorporating it can add even more space and light. I have seen a small row house transformed from dark and drab to light and spacious simply by removing the long hallway and knocking down the wall between the old living room and kitchen/diner. The kitchen was fitted into the space under the stairs, hidden from the main part of the room by a latticework screen.

When you open up rooms in this way, remember to plan doorways. In a kitchen/living/dining room combination, you will need an access door into the room (unless you have removed the hallway) and a door from the kitchen to the outside if you live on the ground floor or have a balcony.

ORGANIZING THE SPACE

Plan the kitchen first. It should be at one end of the room, not in the middle where it would act as a divider and destroy the open-plan atmosphere you hoped to achieve. The amount of space you use for the kitchen should not be more than one third of the room. Position base cabinets or shelves to mark a division between the kitchen area and the rest of the room. If space is limited, this divider can be used instead of a dining table.

A large, open plan room looks best if the same flooring is used throughout. Vinyl or sealed cork tiles are both good choices as they are hard wearing and easy to clean. Then, all you need do is leave the floor uncovered in the kitchen and use rugs in the dining and living areas.

Make sure that the kitchen is well ventilated so that cooking smells don't gather in

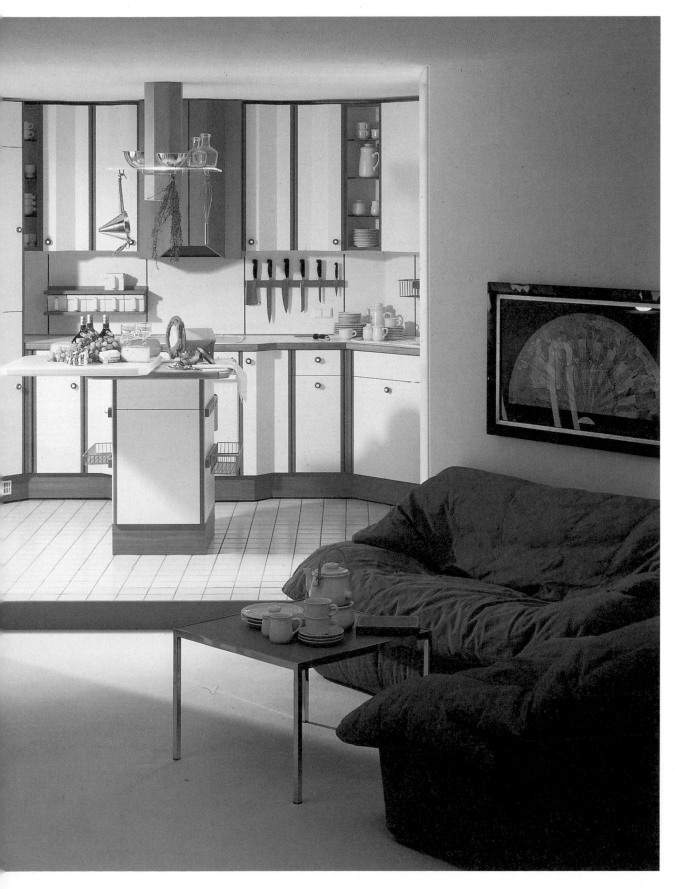

Left: *Try to engineer a smooth transition between the kitchen, with its necessarily functional look, and the softer lines of the living and dining areas. Repeating colors and decorative themes like the brown tones and wood trim in the picture helps to give a uniform effect.*

Free-standing furniture includes mobile bookcases, cupboards and chests, whereas built-in cabinets are in place for good. These do save space and are ideal for awkward and unused spaces but they are expensive.

Modular systems include shelving and cupboards that can be added on to as and when you need the extra storage space (and can afford them). These units can be bought in knock-down packs for do-it-yourself assembly or custom-built for you. Or you may even prefer to design and build your own.

SHELVING

Shelving is really the staple form of storage. It comes in endless shapes and sizes, with varying adjustability. You can choose from metal, wood, even plastic in a variety of finishes, widths and lengths. The best place to look for shelves is the home improvement stores.

In older homes, alcoves on either side of the chimney breast can be fitted with shelves.

MODULAR STORAGE

These units can be added to as you go along, they are easily arranged and very mobile, so you can move them from room to room quite easily. Perhaps the simplest form is a cube system, based on simple wooden or plastic boxes which can be either open or shelved. The contents can then be concealed behind fronts and drawers or left on display. Open cubes can make a versatile and attractive form of storage for TV and stereo. They can also provide an appealing focal point to a room or act as a room divider. In this case take care that an unsightly array of trailing cords don't spoil the desired effect – or worse, become a hazard.

Many different combinations are possible. Some lines offer a wide selection of base units including cabinets with transparent or opaque doors, adjustable shelves, drawer units and open-down tops. Quality units that are properly made should be well finished at the backs so that you can place them at right angles and use them as room dividers. If you can only afford cheaper modular furniture, this can be dramatically improved by applying a couple of coats of paint or by replacing the door handles with something superior or more original. Interior details are very important. Many options are available, so, look for drawers, shelves, wire trays, cassette racks and tape boxes if you know you are going to use them.

Below: *Simple stacking cubes are available ready made with a number of different interior fittings, or you can build your own using laminate-coated chipboard.*

CHILDREN'S PARAPHERNALIA

Remember that anything that stores toys and games for children must be placed at a lower height if it is going to be accessible to them. If you keep everything out of reach you will spend your whole time being asked to get things down for them.

As children get older they often become fascinated by minutiae. Compartmentalized storage, such as tins, small wicker baskets, glass jars and narrow shelves are perfect for when they get to this age. Otherwise just use a little imagination to adapt conventional forms of storage to their needs.

Shelving: Adjustable shelving is a wise choice for coping with the constant build-up of children's toys and general clutter. Giant low-level shelves can be used as seating as well as providing a place to store toys and later books and games. Low-level cupboards with an assortment of boxes placed inside them can be used to contain all sorts of things from puzzles to marbles. The higher shelves can be used to display anything you don't want the children to get their hands on!

Boxes: Perhaps the most fun idea for storage is to use large primary-colored plastic boxes that can be stacked. These are wipeable – an important consideration. Or use a pine blanket box to store children's things in – these can be bought new from furniture shops or picked up quite cheaply from junk shops. If you can fit them with castors it will be much easier to move them from one room to another. Even a rough plank chest can be resuscitated by sanding and a good coat of pretty colored paint, but make sure that you don't leave any nasty splinters to catch on little hands. If you have time and inspiration you could paint them with your child's favorite storybook character or animal. Stencils are another nice idea – and perhaps more fitting if you are going to keep the box in the living room. Another idea is to keep an old picnic basket or other large wicker basket in which to scoop up children's toys, or even an old-fashioned metal steamer trunk. These can be painted in lively colors.

Carts: A form of mobile storage, carts are a good idea for storing children's things as they can be brought out during the day when the children are playing in the living room and wheeled back into the bedroom at bedtime – or when unexpected visitors arrive. In summer you'll even be able to wheel them out into the garden.

Above: *Encourage children to keep their toys tidy by providing brightly colored plastic storage boxes or a wicker chest for quick, easy clearing away at the end of the day. The boxes can be stored inside living room cupboards.*

ALTERNATIVES

Ask yourself what kind of look you want to create and whether you need mobility. A good alternative to traditional storage is office-type storage such as filing cabinets, revolving racks, peg boards and even wire mesh merchandise baskets. If used imaginatively they can be used to create an unusual and inexpensive chic.

Other alternative display systems include lazy Susans, carts on castors and swivel shelves. Some manufacturers offer shelving on a pivot base so that the television can be turned to face the wall when not in use. Carts allow the TV to be wheeled away and transported to another room; both high-tech tubular steel models and wooden country-look designs are available.

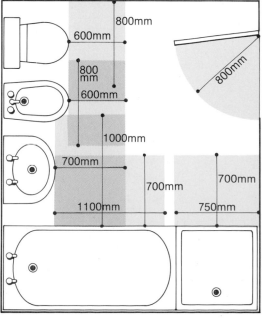

Above: *This spacious modern bathroom features attractive fixtures in gray with maroon trim. Towels and accessories have been chosen to blend in with this color scheme.*

Left: *Wood paneling has given this small bathroom a touch of class. Gold taps and hanging plants complete the effect.*

Far left: *When designing a bathroom make sure you allow sufficient space for everything – including the door. Our plan shows the recommended spaces for each piece of equipment.*

Right: *A bold color scheme is a quick way to revamp a bathroom. Here costs are kept to a minimum as only one row of tiles is used with the rest of the walls sponged in a low-cost paint.*

in ceramic ware in colors to match the bath.

Washbasins come as wall-mounted, pedestal or vanity designs. In a small bathroom, a wall-mounted or vanity model looks neater and plumbing can be hidden in a panel behind which will also serve as a shelf. A vanity model is always useful because a cabinet built around it adds storage space. There are various size basins, ranging from tiny corner-mounted shapes suitable for a powder room or bedroom, to one big enough to double as a baby bath.

Toilets and bidets are available either free standing or wall mounted. In a freestanding model, the unit is screwed to the floor. The wall-mounted version is neater because the unit is mounted on a bracket hidden inside a partition (known as a duct). The water and waste connections and the toilet tank are also concealed behind the duct, giving a neat, space-saving finish. If you install a recess above the duct, it can be used for storage or to make a focal point for the room.

Toilets are also available in water-saving models. These toilets use about 3½ gallons per flush, as opposed to 5 gallons for a standard toilet. Other special toilets include low-profile, extra-gusset and corner models.

Think carefully about who will be using the bathroom when choosing fixtures, especially if there are small children or an elderly or disabled person in the family. A step up to the bath will make climbing in and out easier for toddlers and adds an interesting feature. A separate shower cubicle means that children can wash safely, unattended, but the shower must be a thermostatically controlled type with a preset temperature a child can't easily alter. Thermostatic control prevents a rush of hot or cold water if a tap is turned on elsewhere in the house. A non-slip shower mat fitted in the base of the bath and shower is another safety precaution – and a must in the case of children, the elderly and the infirm.

Installing two basins is sensible if you have children of any age as it eases the strain at peak times. You could set one basin at a lower level, or provide a stool.

As children have a habit of locking themselves in the bathroom or toilet, install a lock that can be opened with a screwdriver from the outside.

It is easy to adapt a domestic bathroom for use by a disabled or infirm person. Install grab handles on the wall beside the bath and toilet and inside the shower cubicle and make sure all floors are non-slip. The elderly, or anyone suffering from rheumatism,

arthritis or the effects of a stroke may find ordinary twist faucets difficult to operate, so install levers instead. Most bathroom manufacturers now include lever taps in their brassware range. If a member of the family is wheelchair bound and cannot use the bath, install a shower with a built-in seat, grab handles and an entrance wide enough to admit the chair. Many bathroom manufacturers now offer shower cubicles designed for the disabled.

PLANNED STORAGE

Organizing bathroom storage can be a real headache, partly because most bathrooms are short on space, and because of the variety of things the average family uses in the bathroom. Toiletries, soaps, medicines, shaving equipment, tissues, cotton, makeup and bath toys can quickly clutter basin and bath surrounds, so organized storage is a must.

The ever-inventive Germans have a ready-made answer with built-in bathroom furniture, a natural development from the kitchen. Cabinets are planned and installed around fixtures and include heated areas for towels, locking sections for medicines, pull-out baskets for dirty linen and many other features. If your budget won't stretch to custom-built storage, installing shelves above the bath and setting the washbasin into a vanity cabinet can help. Putting a skirt of fabric around a

wall-hung basin is a quick and inexpensive way to make a hiding place for cleaning materials, but has drawbacks as the materials will quickly become wet and dirty. Think about setting a basin into a chest of drawers or an old-fashioned marble-topped washstand as an original way to add storage space. If the bathroom is big enough, an old-fashioned pine wardrobe or a dresser will look good and hold towels, toiletries and toys. A corner cupboard is useful because it does not occupy much space but will accommodate a surprising number of bottles, jars and boxes.

At a simpler level, a tier of wire baskets on wheels is a convenient way to house toiletries or you could erect industrial shelving brackets with wire baskets as shelves for a high-tech look. A stacking tier of plastic vegetable storage boxes is useful for bath toys. A couple of hooks or rods near the hand basin will cope with towels and robes. But for safety's sake you should never fit hooks on the inside of a door.

COLOR SCHEMING

Color can affect the overall look of your bathroom as much as shape. Most bathroom manufacturers provide accurate color samples so that you can match fixture shades to wallcoverings and flooring. If the room is small, then an all-around pale color scheme will help to give a feeling of space. Avoid

Left: *Kitchen cabinet doors were used to build this vanity around the washbasin. Cabinet doors come in many different finishes and styles and can be painted, stenciled or stained.*

If the bathroom is very small, think carefully about replacing the tub with a shower stall. A shower takes up approximately 1 square yard of floor space, can be installed in all sorts of odd corners and is faster and more economical to use than a bath. Shower enclosures are available with sliding, corner-entry or curved doors and can be sloped to fit under an attic ceiling or staircase recess. Replacing the tub with a shower may free enough space to have a double basin or to add a bidet. For a tiny space, steal an idea from Scandinavians and build a "wet room". The walls and ceiling are tiled and instead of a shower floor, the entire tiled floor slopes slightly toward the center so that water can drain away through a grille. The shower is mounted on the wall without partitions or drapes to take up valuable space. Most wet rooms contain a small corner-mounted washbasin and a toilet. To use the room, you simply walk in, close the waterproof glass door and switch on the shower. Because every surface is tiled, water drains away quickly. The wet room is an excellent way to hose down muddy children and dogs, as grubby foot- and handprints are washed away by the water. You can build a wet room, complete with corner basin, in a space only 4 feet square.

A vanity cabinet built around the washbasin, and a wall-hung toilet and bidet with pipes concealed behind panels will help to make a small bathroom look neater.

Mirrors are an infallible way to make a small bathroom look larger and lighter. A wall of mirrors at the end of the bathtub will make the room seem twice as long. Acrylic mirror won't steam up and will save you a lot of mopping and cleaning.

Avoid fussy detail and dark colors, as both will make a small room seem even smaller. Choose white or pastel-colored fixtures and a wallcovering that will reflect light. Expensive, shiny foil wallpaper can look stunning when used where it will catch natural light from the window. Install a neat glass shower door instead of untidy curtains.

Use odd spaces and corners for storage units. Narrow shelving doesn't occupy much space and can be concealed with sliding or bi-fold doors. Stick to white to achieve maximum effect.

Replacing the door into the room with a pocket model can free useful wall space for a basin, bidet or toilet. A towel rail mounted on the back of a conventional door is another way to save wall space, or you can hang the towels on the wall above the bathtub, where they are easily within reach.

Left: *Another compact bathroom using every inch of available space. A mirror has been used along the top of one wall to give the illusion of an extra dimension.*

143

MAKE DO AND MEND

The bathroom should be warm, comfortable, even luxurious; a place to relax and soak away the stresses and strains of the day. If you are starting from scratch, comfort can be your prime consideration when choosing fixtures and accessories. But what if you've inherited a chilly, uncomfortable bathroom, and you don't have the funds to replace the existing fixtures? If the plumbing is in good working order but the fixtures chipped or in a color you dislike, rescue is possible. Chips on a bath can be retouched with epoxy paint, or fixtures can be recolored by a specialty bath restoration company. Look in your local directory for the names of companies. Some can apply patterns and special metal or pearlized effects.

If the bath is an old-fashioned footed type and is not boxed in, painting the sides can give a bright new look. Stenciling is easy and adds an individual touch. Stencils can be bought from art and craft shops, or you can make your own designs by cutting shapes from stiff cardboard. Allow each section of the design to dry before applying the next color. Use an enamel paint for best results.

BOXING IN THE BATH

Boxing in an old bath can help to give the bathroom a built-in look. If you are retiling the walls, a tiled bath surround will give a built-in feel. It is better if you can move the surround out slightly from the sides of the bath so that there is a shelf all around. Build a framework first, then box it in with plywood or hardboard. If you are using a mix of plain and patterned tiles, run a line of pattern around the top edge of the bath surround. Louver doors or replacement kitchen cabinet doors or tongue and groove paneling is a good, inexpensive choice if you like the look and feel of wood. Buy plain louvers and stain or paint them the color you want. Wooden replacement kitchen cabinet doors can be stained to look like mahogany or pine, stenciled or given a treatment such as rag rolling, sponging or marbling. Seal pine tongue and groove paneling with clear polyurethane and match it with a pine towel rail, soap dish and toothbrush holder.

For a luxury feel, carry carpet up from the floor to cover the side of the tub. Alternatively, cover the bath panels with washable vinyl wallcovering. If the bath has a hardboard panel, paint it the color of your choice, then make fake panel sections with doweling. Wallpaper inside the paneled sections and paint the panel edging in a deeper

shade to match both the main paintwork and the predominant color in the wallcovering. You can extend this effect to a plain door. Hiding the bath behind a curtain is an economical, trouble-free solution. Hang a rail from wall to wall above the bath and use it to support swathes of filmy drapery, tied back in the center with wide satin ribbon or a circlet of silk flowers. Add a cane chair with some lace cushions, a deep pile carpet, some plants and pretty accessories for instant romance. A jungle of plumbing beneath the washbasin looks unattractive and makes the bathroom feel utilitarian. Boxing the basin in, with a countertop above and louver or replacement doors below, hides the pipes and makes storage space for toiletries and cleaning materials. Hanging a skirt of fabric below the washbasin is a pretty idea but not very practical as the fabric quickly becomes wet.

Changing the color or covering of the walls can provide an instant facelift for a shabby bathroom. If one or two tiles are damaged, they can be replaced, either with matching tiles if available, or with a contrasting or complementary tile in plain or pattern. Look around junk shops for Victorian and Edwardian tiles as their elaborate and colorful patterns look particularly good set into a wall of plain tiling. To remove a damaged ceramic tile, drill into the center using a drill bit recommended for masonry or ceramics. Wear goggles to protect your eyes as the tile may splinter. The tile will crack around the drilled hole. Insert a small screwdriver into the hole and use it to lever the old pieces of tile away from the wall. When the area is clear, remove any traces of old adhesive, then apply fresh tile adhesive and install the new tile.

If you dislike the color or pattern of tiles, it is possible to either paint or retile over the top. To paint tiles, wash well with TSP or a similar cleanser to remove all traces of grease and grime. When the tiles are dry, paint over with a coat of alkyd semigloss paint. Top with gloss. If the tiles are in a strong color, you may need to apply two or three coats of base paint before the gloss.

To tile over tiles, spread the old tiling with tile cement, using a ridged spreader to provide a "key", then apply the new tiles on top.

Make a feature of half a tiled wall by adding a band of doweling or a dado rail above the top row of tiles. Paint the wood and wallpaper or paint the wall above to complement the tiles. There is no rule that says tiles must match. A collection of individual Dutch, Victorian or Edwardian or Mexican tiles is

always effective, or you could experiment with different colored pastels, or a combination of white and one or two primaries in an interesting pattern. Sometimes, tile shops are willing to sell off odds and ends.

Plain painted walls can make a bathroom seem bare and chilly, even if the color scheme is in warm shades. Add interest with a dado rail halfway up, either made from wood or using a wallpaper border. If you look for a coordinated wallcovering range, you can use two different patterns and a dado border either in the middle or about a foot below the level of the ceiling with the second pattern starting immediately above the border and extending over the ceiling.

Less than perfect walls can be hidden by painting first then attaching white garden trellis mounted on slats. Or you could paint the walls and cover them with a display of pictures, framed photographs, china plates, menus or memorabilia. If the bathroom is big enough to stand it, a dramatic color scheme is an inexpensive way to add an individual touch. Try painting the walls glossy black or red, with matching and contrasting towels and accessories. Bathrooms in older homes are often dull and dark. The answer is to paint everything white and cover the floor in either a textured white Indian rug or vinyl tiles. Use cane accessories, mirrors positioned to catch available light and a mass of leafy green

Left: *Old-fashioned fittings are given a new lease on life with a pretty color scheme and traditional mosaic flooring. The walls were painted in soft beige flat latex paint with the ceiling in white. The bath was paneled in, using tongue and groove paneling, then painted to match the walls.*

plants for an airy colonial feel. Stenciling is a simple way to add interest. You could stencil a garland of leaves and flowers around the door or window and along the edge of the bath, or cheat and use wallpaper border instead.

Many modern bathrooms are functional and clean but lacking in character. A few little touches can make all the difference. Add a couple of shelves for books, pretty bottles or colored soaps, bath salts and cotton balls in jars. Buy a quilted box to hold tissues, or make one yourself. A small basket lined with fabric is an attractive way to store toiletries and you can add matching borders to towels. If you are good at needlework, embroider posies of flowers on towels, washcloths and bathrobes. Most needlework shops sell transfers. Look for interesting Victorian or Edwardian bathroom accessories, such as a pitcher and a basin set, a shaving bowl or a pair of china candlesticks. If your taste is modern, a few stunning, brightly framed prints or a crackle glaze or spattered vase will help to add the personal touch.

Plants give an instant facelift and add character and most thrive in warm, humid bathroom conditions. Plants need good light so if the bathroom is dark, you must keep the lights on for part of the day. A lush fern will thrive hanging from the ceiling above the tub, as rising steam creates ideal conditions for this plant.

important types of storage. Provide wide shelves for records and narrow ones for cassettes and computer disks. If closet space is a problem, think carefully about the future of the room before you add a custom-built closet system. Teenagers eventually leave home and those expensive closets will be extraneous. A wheeled hanging rail is a sensible, cost-conscious solution. Girls will appreciate a well-lit makeup mirror. Once again, two of the three-drawer chests and worktop bought for the nursery can come into play, this time as a makeup table. Both sexes will need a full-length mirror.

A desk or big work surface for study is an essential. Add a clip-on light, office filing trays and some containers for pens and pencils. You may need to add electrical outlets for extra lighting, computer, stereo and tele-

vision. For safety's sake, make sure there is an outlet for each appliance. Adaptors can be dangerous if too many are used. Lighting should be flexible. Recessed ceiling spots controlled by a dimmer switch will take care of general light. Add clip-on flexible lamps around work and dressing areas and by the bed for night reading.

Most teenagers will have strong views on how the room should be decorated and will appreciate being allowed to choose color schemes and upholstery. Remember that this is your child's private space and listen to ideas – within reason. It can be tempting to give in for the sake of peace – but you as parents will have to pay for materials and cope with repair and redecorating when the fad for all-black walls or a giant mural of the current pop favorite has passed.

Above: *A boy's room can be modern and functional, especially if it is to combine a hobby or homework area as here. Crisp, clean lines in bright yellow and dove gray give an uncluttered, high-tech look.*

ROOM FOR ONE MORE

Almost everyone enjoys having friends and family to stay, but in many homes, finding the space for a guest room means that those who live there all the time are more crowded than is necessary.

Unless you have the luxury of space to spare, a room which is used only a few times a year is a waste of resources. Think of the many ways in which the room could become part of everyday life, for hobbies, homework, as an extra den, or a play area. This doesn't mean friends and family can't come to visit; with clever planning, the guest room can quickly change roles from family space to extra bedroom.

A convertable sofa will make the room more adaptable than a conventional bed. Choose a good-quality model with a good, thick sprung mattress. The bed should be easy to open and close – test it out in the store first. If the room is to double as a work space, choose furniture which has space for storage of clothes and a worksurface. The simplest way is to position two three-drawer chests about 3 feet apart from each other, then place a laminate or wooden worksurface across the top. The worksurface can be used as a dressing table when friends visit – simply add a free-standing mirror.

Guests will need somewhere to hang their clothes – and you will find the extra closet space useful. There is no need to go to the expense of a custom-built closet system. It is easier, and cheaper, to partition off part of the room with louver or mirror doors and position a shelf and hanging rail inside. A space as small as 6 inches wide is perfectly adequate.

My own guest room, once a sort of dumping ground that had to be hastily cleared when friends were expected, has recently been converted to a bedroom/study and is now used daily for computer games, work, homework and relaxation. The room is small,

Below: *The ideal guest bedroom has ample closet and cabinet space plus a big, comfortable bed. The addition of a small table means that some meals can be taken in the room, giving a luxurious degree of privacy.*

Top and bottom right: *Investing in a sofa bed means tired dinner party guests can stay the night with a minimum of fuss. The sofa bed folds down, and, the table is pushed against the door for privacy.*

around 12 feet by 9½ feet, with windows along one short wall and a door and closet on the other. We planned floor-to-ceiling cabinet storage for one long wall, incorporating a small closet, a computer desk and shelving, then carried the shelving around under the window, spaced out with drawers and another work area. A sofa bed, bedside chest and lamp occupy the second long wall. This easy-to-copy idea can be adapted to almost any space big enough to house a folding bed. We made the cabinets from laminate-faced chipboard but it is possible to buy similar designs ready built.

Although you will probably read suggestions that guests can be accommodated on a sofa bed in the living room, dining room or hall, most people find this sort of arrangement absolutely apalling for any more than one night, and completely lacking in privacy. If you want to have people stay, do try and find a private space for them, safe from the early morning attentions of your dog, cat or boisterous children.

If you entertain regularly, it may be worth having the attic space converted, or adding a ground floor bedroom/study with its own bathroom. Both these rooms will be useful to the family when the visitors have gone.

Try to make the guest room as comfortable as possible. Take a tip from the top hotels and provide a carafe of water and a glass, tea- and coffee-making equipment, a bowl of fruit and some crackers and a selection of magazines and books. Line the drawers with pretty paper and hang scented sachets in the closet. Add some plastic bags for dirty clothes, a needle and a selection of thread, cotton balls, tissues, soap and thick, warm towels; they will all be appreciated. Don't forget a waste basket, and a clock that tells the time accurately. Make sure that the curtains or blinds are easy-to-pull and will meet in the middle. Check the efficiency of the heating or air conditioning in the guest room too. This kind of hospitality is a compliment to your guests that will never go out of fashion.

BATHING FACILITIES

A separate guest bathroom is a luxury which comes low on the list of home priorities but a shower cubicle hidden behind a closet door, or tucked into a corner is easy to install if there is a water supply nearby. If space is really limited, a corner-mounted basin will provide enough space for brushing teeth, shaving , washing hands, etc.

Left: *This totally self-contained compact kitchen is ideal for small attics, studio apartments and offices.*

Right: *Storage space in the kitchen is of prime importance. Here, tall cabinets offer maximum space and the large refrigerator with built-under freezer and combination of microwave and combi-oven are perfectly placed.*

Preparation and storage space: Preparation space is important, whatever your culinary plans. An arrangement which runs oven and cooktop, workspace, drainer and sink (with dishwasher beneath drainer), counter, refrigerator and a storage cabinet is efficient. Install as many wall cabinets as possible for storage of pots, pans and non-perishable foods. If you are working under a strict budget, open shelving can be used. Midway shelves between the counter and wall cabinets make good use of normally wasted space and can be used for salt, pepper and herbs that need to be close at hand. Remember that sliding or tambour doors are easier to use in a confined space than the conventional outward opening type.

Some kitchen manufacturers offer all-in-one kitchens which include a sink, refrigerator and stove, planned into one big unit. Some are designed to fit inside a cupboard, others to be part of the room. Most specialists are happy to design a kitchen for a studio or one-room apartment, a good solution if the space is small or awkward.

WHERE TO PUT THE KITCHEN

However well planned and efficient your mini-kitchen is, there will be times when you won't want it on view. Most cooks hate being watched as they work and would rather guests didn't see what goes on behind the scenes. There are days too, when sheer tiredness means you would rather leave the dishes until morning and won't want to see the clutter as you attempt to relax.

Siting the kitchen depends on the shape of the room. An alcove, or the short leg of an L-shape are both good locations. In a long, narrow room, locate the kitchen at one end, and hide it with bi-fold or sliding doors, or a ceiling-mounted Venetian blind. If there is space, use open shelving three quarters of the way across the kitchen space, or build a narrow base cabinet with shelving or a collection of leafy green plants on top. Both of these ideas will add an interesting feature to the living side of the room.

VENTILATION AND LIGHTING

Good ventilation is vital if you cook, live, eat and sleep in the same room. If possible, locate the kitchen where there is an openable window. A ventilation system at the cooktop will clear cooking smells before they can linger. The system can either be an overhead hood, which sucks cooking fumes up and

Food storage: Refrigeration is essential for healthy, hygienic storage of perishable foods. The size of refrigerator depends on your needs. If all you want to store is milk and the odd piece of cheese, then a small, apartment-size model is fine. If you want to store more, choose a larger one. Frozen foods are quick and convenient for students or working singles, so make sure the unit has ample freezer space for your needs. In tight kitchens, consider separate small under-counter refrigerator and freezer. However, if you rely heavily on frozen foods, at least during the working week, you may find it essential to have a refrigerator with a large freezer section. Collect as many manufacturers' brochures as you possibly can and then, having gotten a good idea of the range available, go to a large department store with a good choice of models, or an appliance showroom, and find a salesperson qualified to answer any remaining queries before you make a final choice. This is a purchase you are going to rely on a lot, so get it right!

You will also need a well-ventilated cupboard for the storage of vegetables and other foodstuffs. Cans and packages can go into wire baskets mounted on the inside of the cupboard door.

Dishwashing: If you can afford it, invest in a dishwasher. A space-saving dishwasher won't take up too much space will help you to keep the kitchen area tidy and free from clutter as dirty dishes can be put out of sight immediately. Otherwise there's a tendency to think it not worthwhile washing a few items, and they accumulate!

If a dishwasher is beyond your means, look for a good, deep sink and mount a drip rack above it. A double sink is a waste of space; look instead for a single-bowl model, possibly with a slide-over chopping board. A garbage disposer installed in the sink will prevent you from carrying bags of garbage through the apartment and down the stairs, and will help to keep the kitchen fresh smelling by getting rid of food remains instantly.

vents them outside, or a down-draft model, a low-profile system that draws the fumes down through the appliance body and then out.

The kitchen area needs a different type of lighting from the part of the room used for living. A ceiling-mounted spotlight track will allow you to beam bright light where it is needed. Small fluorescent strips fitted beneath wall cabinets or shelves can be used to light the worktop areas. Good lighting is an essential when you are working with sharp knives or pouring boiling liquids from one container into another. For safety's sake don't try to manage with just a single overhead light that casts shadows.

DECOR

Kitchen decor must, of course, be practical and easy to clean. As the kitchen is part of a larger room, the color schemes should complement one another. Wallcovering quickly becomes dirty in the steamy environment of the kitchen, so paint or tiles are a better choice. All-over tiling can make a small space look like a public lavatory, so compromise with tiles between counter and wall cabinets and paint in a complementary color elsewhere.

Simple white tiles always look good, and will live happily with changes of decor in the main room. You may be tempted to choose tiles in a very definite color or pattern because they match the wall treatment in the main part of the room, but this will restrict your choice of decor.

The flooring should be warm, comfortable and easy-to-clean. Carrying carpet through from the main part of the room is not a practical idea as it will quickly become shabby and stained by inevitable spillages. Cork or vinyl tiles or vinyl sheet flooring are all warm, quiet and easy-to-clean and will suit most styles of decoration.

A PLACE TO EAT

Although you will probably want a dining area in the main part of the room, it is useful to have an area for solo snacks and light meals in the kitchen. Using a base cabinet and countertop as a room divider creates a space that can be used as a breakfast bar if the divider is built so that there is room to tuck a stool beneath the top. Some kitchen cabinet manufacturers offer pull-out tables built into base cabinets, or you can build a folding flap table against the wall.

Left: *This versatile kitchen divider cabinet combines a variety of useful functions. Notice the slide-out breakfast bar, the shelves of different widths and heights and the storage cabinets, all stacked efficiently in the same unit.*

Above: *If your dining area is small, use mirror tiles on one wall to give the effect of an extra dimension. A glass-topped dining table creates a spacious effect too, as it appears to take up less space than a solid one would.*

THE BATHROOM

Most ready-built one-room apartments and studios have a small separate bathroom. It is more than likely that the bathroom provided with a studio or one-room apartment will be too small for anything more than the bare essentials. If it is your own space, there are various ways to make even a gloomy box cheerful and comfortable. Carpeting the floor is a good start. Use proper bathroom carpeting with a waterproof backing. Cover one wall with mirror, paint the others white and add some healthy green plants for instant light and an airy feel. Thick towels, a heated towel rail and a smart shower door instead of shabby shower curtains are quick and easy brighteners.

If you are converting former warehouse space into loft living quarters, you will probably have to create a bathroom from scratch. This affords you the opportunity to go to town (budget permitting) with separate tub and shower, generous storage and any multi-purpose elements you desire. You will likely already have a small bathroom, with toilet and sink, which should form the basis of your new bathroom simply because rerouting the plumbing is a formidable expense. A space planner can offer invaluable advice.

Adding a new one-room apartment, either for use by teenagers, as a guest suite or a grandparent's apartment, gives you the opportunity to plan a bathroom designed to make the best of minimum space. Local building regulations will dictate the distance and number of doors required between the bathroom and kitchen/living area, so check these first before deciding on a convenient position for the bathroom.

The bathroom will need to be divided from the main part of the room by partition walling or a folding door. The amount of space you partition off depends on how big the room is, but it is possible to fit a lot of bathroom equipment into a remarkably small area – as you will see in our plan showing a bathroom only 5½ feet long by 4½ feet wide. Remember that a shower takes up much less space than a bath and enclosures come in curved shapes, with corner-entry and sliding doors or can be custom-built to fit under a sloped attic ceiling. If you feel that you can't live without a tub, a continental sit-up bath is a better choice than a short-length standard bath as it will allow you to wallow up to your chest in water in about half the amount of space. Add a shower attachment for hair washing and for the days when there isn't

WALLCOVERINGS AND PAINT

The following companies offer customer
   literature.

Ameritone Paint
P.O. Box 190
Long Beach, CA 90801

Laura Ashley
714 Madison Avenue
New York, NY 10021

Charles Barone, Inc.
9505 W. Jefferson Boulevard
Culver City, CA 90230

Clarence House
111 Eighth Avenue, Room 801
New York, NY 10011

Du Pont De Nemours
1007 Market Street
Wilmington, DE 19898

Fashion Wallcoverings
4005 Carnegie Avenue
Cleveland, OH 44103

General Tire & Rubber Company
979 Third Avenue
New York, NY 10022

S. M. Hexter
2800 E. Superior Avenue
Cleveland, OH 44114

F. Schumacher & Company
939 Third Avenue
New York, NY 10022

Sinclair Paints & Wallcoverings
2500 S. Atlantic Boulevard
Los Angeles, CA 90040

Albert Van Luit & Company
4000 Chevy Chase Drive
Los Angeles, CA 90039

WINDOWS

Anderson Corporation
P.O. Box 12
Bayport, MN 55003

Caradco Windows & Doors
Division of Scoville Manufacturing Company
1098 Jackson Street
Dubuque, IA 52001

Lord & Burnham
P.O. Box 225
Irvington, NY 10533

Marvin Windows
Warroad, MN 56763

Pella Windows
100 Main Street
Pella, IA 50219

Southern Cross Lumber & Millwork
143 Brown Road
Hazelwood, MO 63042

INDEX